KIA WHITE

A Rainbow In The Desert

First published by Celeste Publishing 2025

Copyright © 2025 by Kia White

All rights reserved. No part of this publication may be reproduced, stored or transmitted in any form or by any means, electronic, mechanical, photocopying, recording, scanning, or otherwise without written permission from the publisher. It is illegal to copy this book, post it to a website, or distribute it by any other means without permission.

Kia White asserts the moral right to be identified as the author of this work.

First edition

ISBN: 9780999325667

This book was professionally typeset on Reedsy.
Find out more at reedsy.com

To my husband Brian and daughter Bria. You two are promises fulfilled.

Contents

Foreword	ii
Chapter 1: The Desert	1
Chapter 2: I Have Learned-Life Experienced	5
Chapter 3: Grief & Loss	7
Chapter 4: And God Remembered Me	10
Chapter 5: Nothing Wasted	15
Chapter 6: Trusting God	18
Chapter 7: In Due Season	22
Chapter 8: A Promise Fulfilled	26

Foreword

Have you ever seen a rainbow in the desert? I have. It was the most breathtaking phenomenon I have ever witnessed. My husband and I were on our way to our honeymoon. From the sky, we saw it clear as day. He said, "you have to take a picture of this" and I'm so glad I captured that moment, it was a rare glimpse of a true manifestation of God's promise. It was as if God was literally showing us a visual representation of how wonders can happen. When you think of a rainbow, it's usually after rain, however; we were flying above the desert. There was no rain in sight. There was an overcast and not much sun and yet we saw a beautiful rainbow below.

In the Bible, the rainbow represents God's promises. That He will keep them and He will fulfill them. The rainbow first appears in The Bible toward the end of the story of the worldwide flood in Genesis 6-9. The wooden ark kept Noah, his family, and many animals safe when God caused rain to fall for 40 days and nights and flood the entire earth. God did this because of the evil and wickedness of humankind (Genesis 6:5-12).

God made this promise, signified by the rainbow, not only to people but to "every living creature... the birds, the livestock and all the wild animals, all those that came out of the ark... every living creature on earth" (Genesis 9:9-10). The covenant is perpetual for all generations. Never again will there be a worldwide flood. Never again will God destroy the earth with flood waters. The rainbow represents God's covenant to His chosen people, that if He made a promise, He will make good on it. His word will not return to Him void, but it will accomplish that which He pleases and it will prosper where He sent it.

The rainbow was an impression placed by God in the sky that He will fulfill His promises for not only a generation, but generations to come. When I saw this rainbow while I was on the way to my honeymoon, this was confirmation that I was in alignment with God's will for my life. Following a storm or heavy rainfall, a rainbow is a nearly certain sight in nature. Just as during prosperous times, we anticipate continued success, and the seamless unfolding of events strengthens our faith in God. We're familiar with God's rainbows following storms, but what if he placed one in a desert? Consider this: deserts symbolize barrenness, aridity, lack of growth, and stagnation. How then can a rainbow appear in such a place? I will tell you how. I serve an amazing God that even in a season of not feeling like He will fulfill His promises or in a place where it does not look like the promise will come to pass, God is still faithful to perform His work. Environmental factors and conditions are irrelevant to God's promises. It does not matter what it looks like. It does not matter what you are up against because His promises are Yes and Amen.

I felt like a rainbow in the desert for years. I was a walking billboard and testimony of God's faithfulness, yet my environment sometimes felt like a desert, barren and unfruitful. I served God's people even when I was hurting or felt mistreated; I still showed up. I served God's people through disappointments and discouragement, and God continued to bless me financially and spiritually. After attending a powerful service or ministering to others, sometimes I would come home to an empty house feeling like God forgot about me. "Am I doing something wrong?" I would ask God during my time of prayer. "Am I in alignment?" It was doing those times that God would not speak right away. Instead, He would answer me through impressions, dreams or His audible words, but it was not always immediate.

I believe God was teaching me how to exercise my faith and just when I would think, well maybe God didn't say that or maybe I missed something, He would show me He was not like a human. He does not lie, but He is a keeper of promises. This book is about all the times God kept and continues to keep His promises even in the most unusual circumstances. May reading this inspire you, and may you hold on to God's promises, even when they seem unlikely to be fulfilled.

Chapter 1: The Desert

There is no place quite like Arizona. The southern region of Arizona is largely a desert. You may ask, what is so great about a desert? A place that is dry, desolate, or even barren. Well, when I first visited the state, I developed an immediate affinity for the place. The month was November and it was 70 degrees. I thought this feels like spring in the winter. Then there was the vastness of the mountains that reminded me of how big God is. They were a sight to see and while riding in the car on the highway, a spectacular feeling of peace and wonder came over me. Suddenly I embraced the unknown of what was ahead of my life. A feeling of maybe all the things I have been praying, fasting and believing God for will happen.

I didn't realize it, but now I see that witnessing the breathtaking beauty of the Arizona mountains was a prophetic moment. God reassured me in this way that my prayers would be answered. He was just going to take me on the scenic route and that route seemed long and strenuous, filled with peaks and valleys. My travels to Arizona began because I needed adventure in my life. For years, I had sacrificed a lot of things for my assignment. Majority of my work in The Lord's church was out of obedience, however; as I reflect, I realized sometimes the money and energy I sacrificed was not because God told me to but was out of obligation or loyalty. Back then, I lacked experience in navigating boundaries and balance in serving in ministry. I am now very clear and assertive in saying no and standing firm on not committing to something if God has not given me the green light.

My routine was getting old and my life felt mundane. I stepped out on faith and booked a flight to travel to a place I had never seen before. I am so glad I did.

Now back to these mountains I saw, God did His best artwork with them. He carved out every peak and valley. He painted them a beautiful brownish red clay like color and to add to their beauty, He placed the sunlight to capture the essence of their appeal. The carving of these mountains took time and that reminded me that God makes everything beautiful in His timing. What a sight to see! Visiting Arizona was the beginning of me changing my perspective about the desert, the barren place I felt I was in. At the time I did not get this revelation but in retrospect seeing the desert from a different lens was part of God's plan. He's so clever. I believe God brought me to the desert for many reasons. One of them was to speak to me clearly and another reason was to test me. The Hebrew word for desert is midbar, which also means "the place of the word." Midbar shares the same root word as dibar, which means the "Holy of Holies."

In my desert place I began to see clearly through the haze and smoking mirrors of life, what was necessary and unnecessary. What was my assignment and what was no longer a part of it. Dreams and prophecies became clearer. Although I did not enjoy the place I was in life, I knew the desert was part of my journey to get to my promised land. What did my desert look like you may ask? I was a single woman, no children, disappointed by the outcome of my dating experience, grieving the loss of my maternal grandmother and my step dad who passed away one week from each other. Their memorial services were also one week from each other. I felt alone, hopeless and anxiety reared its ugly head with a vengeance.

I felt weary in doing well. Despite a godly lifestyle and striving to do everything right, I did not receive the desires of my heart: a husband, a family, and career growth in the time frame I wanted. My prayers were not getting answered and I felt overlooked by God. Then God spoke to me, "this is your reasonable

CHAPTER 1: THE DESERT

service." That's right, I had to check my heart. I felt convicted and pondered, am I living for God just to get what I want or am I doing this because I love Him? God says if you love Me, then you will keep my commandments. Not if I give you what you want, not if I bless you, not if I answer your prayers, but if you love Me. Wow! That moment reminded me of what my walk with God was all about. Love. God is love and if I ever wanted to be successful in any area of my life, I would definitely need to have a mature understanding of God's love. Not the romantic stuff we see on TV or in the movies, but the unconditional love that He has for us and wants us to have. How can I be ready for a husband and family if I did not understand what true love entails?

The scripture Deuteronomy 8:2 comes to mind because it reads "And you shall remember [always] all the ways which the Lord your God has led you these forty years in the wilderness, so that He might humble you and test you, to know what was in your heart (mind), whether you would keep His commandments or not."

Arizona heat can be brutal. As beautiful as the scenery is, it is hard to enjoy in the summer. With temperatures reaching in the triple digits. It is a dry heat, but it is still heat. The winters were mild and felt like spring or fall. These conditions metaphorically remind me that as seasons change, so do the degrees in which we can handle them. In one season Arizona, a desert, was bearable even tolerable and in another it seemed like the temperature was unbearable so unbearable it was hard to embrace the beauty of the place but if you dig deep enough, you will find beauty in the purpose of it all. Again, God makes everything beautiful in His time. Not ours, but His.

He is the potter, and we are the clay. Just as the potter takes the clay and puts it on the shelf to dry to prepare it for the refinery, so does God. He takes us through the desert so we can endure, prevail, and so we can prepare for the transformation. If a potter places clay in the refinery before it has completely dried, the clay will explode. The clay could not handle the fire and God puts us in the desert to dry out what needs to be dried out, then He may turn up the heat to refine us. We think the heat is too much, but the heat is working for us to make us polished and mature for our next level. The heat indicates that after I go through the fire, there will be a promotion, there will be elevation. How is it that we have to go through the scorching heat in the thick of life before we can reach certain levels? The fire makes the clay formidable. It is unbreakable. God wants to make sure that when He fulfills that promise, we will not forget where we came from, we will use the tools He has supplied us with to be unstoppable, immovable and always abounding in His work.

I persevered through it all and endured. I made the best of my situation. The times where I could embrace the beauty of the season I was in, I did. The times where it was hard to find beauty in this journey, I was grateful even for the smallest of things. There were a lot of tears, there was a lot of uncertainty, a lot of disappointment, but also a lot of moments of joy, success, open doors and accomplishments.

Chapter 2: I Have Learned-Life Experienced

The Apostle Paul put it so eloquently when he was letting the Philippines know that whether he is abased or abound, hungry or full he has learned to be content. He even went on to say that he is able to be happy and go on through life and accomplish what needs to be done because it is Christ who strengthens him. The key word is that he learned. Meaning there were some seasons in which there were life lessons that produced character, integrity and discipline. I can wholeheartedly relate to this passage of scripture. There are some things you can learn from other people's journey and then there are some things you just have to go through in order to get the full lesson.

My grandmother, who I affectionately called Grandma Thelma, would always tell me to chalk it up to life experiences when I would express to her my fear of failure or not being able to achieve my goals. Simple advice, yet such a tough concept for me to grasp. Setting out to achieve a goal only for things not to go as I wanted them to just never resonates well with me. In my walk with Christ, I realized I could not operate in the fullness of faith if I was too careful not to "mess up." When situations did not go as I planned, I would be so disappointed, distraught and discouraged. I did not like feeling like a failure. It was embarrassing and humiliating to me. My perspective of failure changed when I realized that just because something does not work out the way I wanted it to or planned, does not mean my labor was in vain. I reflect on a time I was in college, I had my life figured all out. I was going to go to radiology school and work a little bit and then apply for medical school. Imagine my surprise when I received my rejection letter from radiology school. I had a complete meltdown. I was spiraling and could not process my next steps.

All I could do was sit on the floor, scream and cry. I was so afraid of not being accomplished in life. My mom attempted to calm me down, but to no avail. She called my grandma. I cannot recall her precise words of comfort, her conversation left me feeling encouraged. Though this rejection shocked my world, it also opened the door that put me on a completely unique career path that was attached to my destiny. You see, my master plan was not what God wanted. I had to find out what my purpose entailed as well as what He wanted me to do. I did some serious soul searching. With the help of the book <u>Purpose Driven Life,</u> I could navigate that season of obscurity and it led me to the successful career I have today.

Fast forward to life after college and working as a young professional, I could see the hand of God clearly all over that rejection letter. My success in my career is all credited to divine intervention. When God gives you an assignment, sometimes He will close the doors you want to walk through to ensure your pathway is on the straight and narrow. I am blessed that He ordered my steps at that pivotal point in my life. The moral of my story is you can not let rejection discourage you and please do not let your disappointments dim your light or failure forfeit the path God wants you to take. What you may see as unsuccessful is actually part of your path of greatness. Like the Apostle Paul, learn to be content in whatever state you may be in. Know that an academic degree does not define you, a career does not define you and neither does an award, but overall, your strength and the key to your happiness and success is knowing your identity in Christ.

Chapter 3: Grief & Loss

If you have never had to say goodbye or let someone go out of your life, then there is a pain that cuts so deep that you have yet to experience. However, as we live, grief and loss is inevitable. Whether it is ending a relationship, friendship, marriage, or the death of a loved one, grieving is a process in which no one can rush, articulate, or define. You can not drink it away, eat it away, smoke it away, sleep it away, sex it away or spend it away. It sneaks up on you when you least expect it. All the while, you are fighting to remain normal, but part of you has changed and you have to adapt and adjust to life without the person whose company you once enjoyed.

It is a lot to process and although it is difficult and you may experience sad moments, there is beauty in the experience. The Bible says blessed are those who mourn, for they shall be comforted (Matthew 5:4). Meaning, when you lose someone that you cherished so much, those are times when you will know God to be a comforter. He will send people your way to show you kindness. He will provide you with a peace that surpasses all understanding and He will give you strength by providing joy.

In my seasons of grief and loss, I witness the love of God like never before. I had co-workers who I barely had a relationship with show up to funerals as a sign of support or sent me a card. I had friends send care packages and flowers just to show they were thinking of me or take me out to lunch to make sure I did not forget to eat. Bereavement gifts from my family demonstrated their thoughts and prayers. This was the beauty of the experience I discussed in the paragraphs above. Let me be very clear, there is nothing glamorous about grieving, but to see how kind and generous people can be in your most vulnerable moment is humbling and remarkable.

The pain comes in waves, cycles, phases and it is unpredictable. You can be in the bathroom getting ready to start your day and suddenly, a wonderful memory of the person you lost will surface. At that moment, tears or sobbing could follow a smile or laughter. It is a confusing time for sure and you can feel crazy and alone. You should know everyone grieves in their own way and in their own time. There is no timeline or date of completion. It is a marathon, not a sprint. The only difference is you never really reach the finish line, you just learn to adjust, endure and keep moving.

During the time in which I lost my maternal grandmother and my stepfather a week from each other and attending their services a week apart, there was a heaviness that came upon me and it was really difficult for me. It came as a total surprise to me because when my youngest brother died; I thought I knew how to navigate grief, as that was one of the most difficult times of my life.

That time in my life, I learned you are never immune to grief, it's triggering, and it is devastating. Besides losing two people back to back, I was dealing with disappointment in where I was in my life. I was grieving the life I thought I should have had by that time. I thought by a certain time I should be married with kids. I should have my own family. Along with the grief, I had a dating experience that was a complete joke… no; I take that back more like a bad comedy show. It started off with smiles, laughter and then ended abruptly while I was still trying to comprehend the punch line.

Anxiety consumed me. Will this ever happen for me? I began to question what God promised me. I was sad and hopeless. My faith was lacking during one of the most vulnerable moments in my life.

I would have uncontrollable crying spells and an overwhelming feeling of doom and gloom. It is in that season that God sent me comfort through His word. He used people to speak life into me. Tell me I will be a wife, I will be a mother. God sent confirmation after confirmation that I was on the right path. I just had to trust God would make good on His promises.

Chapter 4: And God Remembered Me

You can have it all, just not all at once. When I was single, I did not understand this. My desire to be married and have children was so strong and I was wondering what was taking so long. I would often ask God what I am doing wrong. Where is my husband? Will I ever have kids? As women, we have a biological clock, or at least that is what the world tells us. That biological clock mentality makes us feel as though we are running out of time, which exacerbates anxiety and fear. In hindsight, I now understand why God had me wait. I believe you truly have to establish being self-sufficiently single before you have a healthy relationship. There are things that are easier to accomplish when you are not in a relationship with someone or in a marriage or a parent.

For example, in my single years, I was on my assignment and doing all that God had called me to do. My roles included a full-time career, entrepreneur, health & wellness coach, Zumba instructor, publishing company owner, and author. Despite a fulfilling walk and accomplishing so much, a sense of incompleteness lingered; I knew why. Some things God promised me had not come to pass, and that was a void only He could fill in due season.

It had been 5 years since I went on an actual date and 7 years since I was in a serious relationship. I remember when I came to realize that in order for me to fully walk this journey with God; He had to have my undivided attention. I had not mastered balancing a relationship while simultaneously dedicating my life to Jesus, so I made the radical decision to not date or entertain anyone

CHAPTER 4: AND GOD REMEMBERED ME

until I felt my season of "hiding" was over. Let me clarify what I mean by hiding. God may conceal you to keep you safe. I understood not dating until I felt a release was my conviction and not everybody has the grace to vow to do something like this, but I wanted to prove to God that I was serious in my walk and not playing any games. The keywords are my conviction. You can not try to emulate someone else's journey because you want the results they received. It has to be your conviction. Unless The Lord builds your house, your labor is in vain. The reason behind your why has to be more than appeasing your desires. Pleasing God and seeking Him must be the driving forces behind it. It is difficult to sustain living for God when you do things with the wrong heart posture. I digress. Making this bold decision required me to focus on growing in God. I exercised in godliness by studying His Word, serving in His church, praying and fasting.

As a result, I developed a new mindset. My perspective on life and how I approached it changed. Everything I did was intentional and on purpose. Even down to who I spent my time with, how I spent it, where I spent it, what I watched and the music I would allow my ears to hear. My self-awareness increased regarding my behavior, language, and self-talk. I now understand that what I was experiencing was a season of consecration. Organically, I pressed towards the mark of my higher calling and put the former things behind me.

My priorities changed the closer I got to God. My anxiety about the future lessened as my purpose became clearer. I pursued everything God had planned for me. I started feeling better about myself, more confident and with higher self-esteem. My need for male or worldly approval was gone. When I found my identity in Christ–people, places or things no longer determined my value.

This revelation came with time and experience. When I looked at myself the way God saw me, other people's opinions or judgement didn't matter. This was and still is a powerful place to be. When your confidence comes from God, no one can come in between that. Part of my journey in singleness was learning to love myself and not determining my self-worth on how much attention or gifts I received from a man.

At last! I arrived at a point of self-awareness, understanding my worth and the value of my contributions, much like the woman described in Proverbs 31. My merchandise was and still is good! I was confident and refused to be disrespected by any man who didn't appreciate the woman I'd grown into.

When I first met Brian, I did not realize he would one day become my husband. There was no grand, cinematic moment where our worlds collided, and the heavens opened. We simply met at a collaboration meeting between different organizations. After the meeting, he approached me, introduced himself, and mentioned that he remembered me from high school. To my surprise, I had no recollection of ever crossing paths with him back then.

We laugh about it now, but he had to show me his yearbook to prove it. Sure enough, not only had we attended the same high school, but we had also graduated in the same class—Class of 2002.

There was no instant spark, no butterflies—just a casual introduction and conversation. Afterward, I went on my way, giving it little thought. Months passed, and as the year came to a close, we ran into each other again at another meeting. This time, we exchanged numbers, but the timing wasn't right. We were in different phases of our lives—both of us needing to close certain chapters before we could start a new one. As the saying goes, he was still out in "them streets," and I was entertaining a counterfeit.

Two years later, after we both joined the same Zoom meeting, he reached out to me again. This time, he asked me out, and I accepted. Looking back, I'm so glad I did. That night, our conversation flowed effortlessly. We reminisced about our separate journeys through our twenties, shared stories about our families, and genuinely enjoyed each other's company. From that night on, we were inseparable.

CHAPTER 4: AND GOD REMEMBERED ME

I used to make fun of people who said that they married their best friend. I thought it was really corny and cliché and that they were just saying that because it sounded good. Now I am a witness that you can truly marry your best friend. It's not just a cliché, and it's not just something people say because it sounds good, but it is actually a reality for some people. When you can just spend time with a person all day and genuinely enjoy their company, that is something unique. We don't have to take lavish trips or do anything extravagant. We can just watch a movie, partake in a nature activity, or cook a meal together. These are the simple things that bring us happiness and I don't take those moments for granted.

Before our romance, I was a single Christian woman, childless, and I want to elaborate more about that time of my life. Singleness is a gift they say—that is true for people that have that gift. I did not. Another phrase used was to be content in your singleness. Hearing that advice used to make my eyes roll, especially when it came from married people—it always seemed like only married people were the ones saying it. That insensitive remark, lacking emotional awareness, really bothered me.

Desiring marriage and recognizing it as part of one's journey or destiny—to become a wife or husband—does not automatically mean a person is discontent in their singleness. I think we should normalize empathizing, especially as Believers, with singles who are serious about their walk with The Lord, desire marriage, but haven't yet reached that stage. Perhaps focusing more on preparation and what you do while you're waiting is more constructive than making dismissive statements such as "just be content in your singleness." Let's start approaching these conversations with emotional intelligence by providing practical solutions and examples.

God remembered me in my season of singleness, seeing the desires of my heart and the faithfulness with which I waited with Him. It wasn't always easy, but I remained obedient, trusting that His timing was perfect—even when it didn't align with my own expectations. While I had periods of uncertainty regarding the promise, my faith remained strong. I used my single years to prepare for marriage by focusing on my relationship with God, rather than settling for less or rushing into anything.

In that season, God refined my character, teaching me patience, trust, and contentment. I leaned into His presence, finding joy in serving Him rather than dwelling on what I didn't yet have. My obedience wasn't about earning a blessing but about honoring God with my life, regardless of the circumstances.

Then, in His perfect time, He was faithful. He brought me into marriage, not just with anyone, but with the person He had ordained for me. He confirmed His constant remembrance of me, seeing each tear, prayer, and surrender. His faithfulness didn't stop at marriage; it extended into motherhood, blessing me with the role I had long desired—to nurture and love a child of my own.

Now, as a wife and a mother, I see clearly how God's hand was in every step of my journey. His faithfulness is not just a once in a lifetime event, but a continuous presence in my life. He fulfilled His promises, not because of my striving, but because He is good, and His Word never returns void. Looking back, I can say with certainty that His plan was always greater than mine, and His timing was always right.

Chapter 5: Nothing Wasted

My time serving within the four walls of the church was a journey filled with both highs and lows. If I had to summarize it, I would say it was neither entirely good nor entirely bad—it was a mix of both. Yet, through it all, I remain grateful because God's Word reminds us to give thanks in all things. Every experience, whether joyful or challenging, played a role in shaping the woman I am today. One thing is certain to me now; these pivotal events were purposeful. I experienced some of the most memorable and fulfilling moments of my life while serving in the church. There is something powerful about being part of a faith community, working toward a shared mission, and witnessing lives being transformed by God's love. Serving gave me purpose, direction, and a sense of belonging. I found joy in pouring into others—whether through ministry, outreach, or simply offering encouragement to someone in need.

One of the greatest blessings of serving was the relationships I built. I met people who became lifelong friends, mentors, and spiritual family. We prayed together, worshiped together, and navigated life's challenges as a community. There was an undeniable sense of unity and strength in knowing that we were all striving toward the same goal—spreading the love of Christ and building His kingdom. I cherished many moments spent in prayer meetings, worship nights, and mission trips where I felt God's tangible presence.

Beyond the relationships, serving in the church allowed me to grow spiritually in ways I never expected. It stretched me, challenged me, and deepened my understanding of God's Word. I learned what it meant to lead with humility, to trust God in uncertainty, and to rely on His strength rather than my own. Serving wasn't just about giving—it was also about receiving, as God used those experiences to mold and refine me.

However, my time serving in the church was not without its difficulties. While the community aspect was a blessing, it also brought challenges. The church has imperfect people, and with that comes misunderstandings, disappointments, and sometimes even hurt. I faced moments where I felt unseen, unappreciated, or as though my contributions didn't matter. I often struggled with burnout—giving so much of myself to ministry that I neglected my own well-being.

One of the hardest lessons I learned was that not everyone who serves has pure intentions. I encountered situations where politics, favoritism, and pride played a role in leadership decisions. It was difficult to reconcile the love and grace of God with the imperfections of people in the church. I often questioned whether I was in the right place, wondering if my efforts were truly making a difference.

There were also moments of deep discouragement—times when I felt like I was pouring out so much but receiving little in return. I had to wrestle with my own expectations and understand that my service was ultimately for God, not for people. Even when I felt overlooked, He saw me. Even when I felt weary, He was my strength. Looking back, I realize that every struggle, every tear, every difficult moment was not in vain. Through all the joys and challenges, God was teaching me endurance, patience, and the importance of serving with a pure heart. He showed me that my identity was not in my role or title, but in Him alone. I had to learn to separate my faith in God from my experiences with people. Just because people fail does not mean God does.

One of the greatest lessons I took from that season was the importance of setting healthy boundaries. It's easy to misconstrue that serving means saying "yes" to everything, but God never called us to run ourselves into the ground. I learned that it's okay to step back, to rest, and to protect my peace. My relationship with God had to come before my work for Him.

I also learned the value of discernment—understanding where God was truly calling me to serve rather than simply filling a need. There is a difference between serving out of obligation and serving out of purpose. When I aligned my service with where God was leading me, I found greater joy and fulfillment. Even in the places that were hard, I see now that God was shaping me, strengthening me, and preparing me for what was ahead.

Despite the peaks and valleys, I can confidently say that God was faithful through it all. My time serving in the church played a significant role in shaping who I am today. It taught me resilience, deepened my faith, and prepared me for the seasons that followed—including marriage and motherhood.

Even in the hardest moments, God was using my experiences to refine me. He never wasted a single tear, a single prayer, or a single act of obedience. What I once saw as struggles, I now see as stepping stones—each one leading me closer to the woman He created me to be.

All of it was for my good. The moments of joy, the lessons learned, even the pain. Every encounter, every season, every trial had a purpose. God used it all—both the good and the bad—to shape me for what He had in store. Now, as I reflect on that time, I do so with gratitude, knowing that every experience was part of His divine plan. As I walk in the promises He has fulfilled, I see the bigger picture in my life. I see how He took everything I experienced and used it to build character. For that, I am truly thankful.

Chapter 6: Trusting God

Trusting God in my season of waiting on His promises was not always easy. There were moments of doubt, seasons of silence, and times when I wondered if the very things I prayed for would ever come to pass. In those moments, I had a choice—to either allow waiting to be a time of frustration or a time of preparation. By God's grace, I chose the latter. While waiting on His promises, I consciously spent my time wisely. I didn't just sit idly, hoping for change. Instead, I was intentional about growing, building, and preparing for the life I believed God was leading me into.

In my season of waiting, I accomplished much—things that not only filled my time but also positioned me for the blessings to come. I poured myself into writing, using my words to inspire, encourage, and uplift others. Writing books was more than just an accomplishment; it was a way to express the lessons I was learning and the faith I was holding onto. Each page reflected my journey—the struggles, the victories, the moments of uncertainty, and the unwavering hope I clung to.

Beyond writing, I pursued entrepreneurial endeavors that allowed me to grow both personally and professionally. I took risks, stepped out in faith, and built something meaningful. There's something powerful about trusting God with the vision He places in your heart and taking steps to bring it to life, even when the full picture isn't yet clear. My entrepreneurial journey taught me resilience, patience, and the importance of trusting the process.

CHAPTER 6: TRUSTING GOD

Financial stability was another area where I saw significant growth. I became more intentional about managing my finances, ensuring that I was being a good steward of what God had already placed in my hands. I worked diligently to establish a solid financial foundation, not only for myself but for the future I believed God was preparing for me. As a result, I became more financially stable and improved my credit score, positioning myself for long-term success.

While I focused on tangible achievements, my greatest growth during my waiting season was in my spiritual life. I deepened my relationship with God in ways I never had before. I spent more time in prayer, worship, and studying His Word. The waiting season was not just about achieving external success, but also about becoming the woman God was calling me to be.

During this time, God promoted me to different levels of ministry, becoming an ordained evangelist and later on a pastor. This wasn't something I pursued for titles or recognition—it was a calling that God placed in my heart. Ministry required sacrifice, dedication, and a willingness to serve beyond my comfort. It stretched me in ways I didn't expect, but it also strengthened my faith and deepened my dependence on God.

Becoming an evangelist and pastor in my season of waiting taught me that God prepares us long before we step into the fullness of His promises. He refines us, equips us, and ensures that when the doors open, we are ready to walk through them. The waiting wasn't about delay; it was about development.

Another major milestone I achieved during this season was buying homes. This was not just about acquiring property—it was about establishing a foundation for the future. Each home represented faith in action, trusting that what I was building would one day serve a greater purpose. It was a reminder that even while waiting, we can take steps toward the life God has for us.

Buying homes required discipline, planning, and faith. There were moments when it felt overwhelming, but I knew God was guiding every decision. Looking back, I see how each home was a symbol of God's provision, reminding me He is a promise-keeper. He had already gone before me, making a way even when I didn't fully see it.

One of the greatest lessons I learned in my waiting season is that preparation is a prerequisite. Every skill I developed, every lesson I learned, and every challenge I overcame was part of His divine plan. I used to think waiting was about inactivity, but I learned that waiting on God is an active process. It's a time of preparation, of refinement, and of growth.

I also learned that God's timing is perfect. There were moments when I wanted things to happen faster, when I felt like I was ready for the promises I was believing for. Looking back, I realize that had those promises come sooner, I wouldn't have been prepared to receive them. God wasn't just working on my circumstances—He was working on me. I learned to trust that delays are not denials. Just because something hadn't happened yet didn't mean it wouldn't happen. I had to remind myself that God's promises are yes and amen (2 Corinthians 1:20). Even when I couldn't see it, He was moving behind the scenes, aligning everything according to His perfect plan.

Another powerful lesson was that faith requires action. Believing in something is not enough—we must also take steps toward it. During my season of waiting, I didn't just pray for financial stability; I actively managed my finances. I didn't just hope for a future in ministry; I pursued training and mentorship. I didn't just dream of homeownership; I took practical steps to make it happen. Faith without works is dead (James 2:26), and my waiting season was proof of that truth.

As I stand on the other side of that waiting season, I can see the hand of God so clearly. He was faithful then, and He is faithful now. The things I once prayed for—the things I prepared for—He has brought to pass. Marriage, motherhood, ministry, financial stability—God made good on every promise

CHAPTER 6: TRUSTING GOD

in His perfect timing.

Looking back, I am overwhelmed with gratitude. What once felt like a long and uncertain season was actually a time of divine preparation. God wasted nothing. Not the hard days, not the tears, not the moments of frustration. Every part of my journey was in alignment.I now realize that waiting is not about passively enduring time; it's about actively trusting God, using the season wisely, and preparing for what's ahead. My story is a testament to the fact that when we remain faithful in the waiting, God remains faithful in the fulfillment.

To anyone still in their waiting season, I encourage you—don't waste it. Use this time to grow, to build, to prepare. God is not withholding His promises from you; He is preparing you to receive them. When the time comes, you will step into everything He has for you, knowing that your labor was not in vain.

Chapter 7: In Due Season

"And let us not grow weary in well doing: for in due season we shall reap, if we faint not." — Galatians 6:9

This verse was my anchor when I felt like quitting everything. It was a reminder that no matter how exhausted, uncertain, or overwhelmed I felt, my due season was coming. I was doing a lot—too much. I was constantly on the go, moving from one responsibility to the next, pouring out in every direction. My days were long, starting at 8 a.m. and often not ending until 11 p.m. Some nights, I was so drained that sleep became more of a priority than even eating. Many times, I had to choose: Do I take a nap or eat? Sleep always won.

Beyond the physical exhaustion, there was another weight I carried—the emptiness of coming home to an empty house. It didn't feel lonely; I had built a full and busy life. However, I felt unsettled knowing I would come home to no one. It left me questioning; when would my due season come? I did all the right things. I sowed in faithfulness, obedience, and diligence yet, I wondered when I would finally reap the benefits of my well-doing.

On top of my exhaustion and longing for my promises to manifest, I was also wrestling with something deeper—the fear of missing out. As I looked around at others in relationships, engaged, married, or building families, I couldn't help but feel like time was slipping away from me.

CHAPTER 7: IN DUE SEASON

I wasn't dating in my prime years, and that thought baffled me. Society often tells us that there is a window for love, for marriage, for starting a family, and if you don't seize it, you might miss it altogether. What if all my sacrifice, all my hard work, was for nothing? What if I was so busy that I missed the very thing I desired? I questioned, did God really tell me to do this? Was I truly following His plan, or was I just being self-righteous? Had I convinced myself that I was doing His will when, in reality, I was just running on autopilot?

These questions haunted me during my busiest moments and whispered to me in my quietest ones. I needed clarity. I needed to hear from God in a way that silenced my doubts and reaffirmed my path.In those moments of uncertainty, it became imperative that I fasted, isolated myself, and immersed myself in God's Word. I needed to realign with His voice, to shut out the noise of my thoughts, my fears, and even the well-meaning advice of others.

My seasons of isolation were never long, but they were necessary. They gave me the space to hear God clearly. During these times, I would:

1. Eliminate distractions—social media, unnecessary conversations, and even certain commitments that were draining me
2. Spend intentional time in prayer—not just talking to God, but also listening for His response.
3. Speak His Word over my life—declaring His promises out loud, reminding myself that what He said would come to pass.

It was in these quiet moments that I found clarity. God wasn't withholding anything from me—He was preparing me. God did not delay my due season. Even after gaining clarity, the reality of exhaustion didn't go away overnight. Serving, working, and waiting were still draining, however; the difference was, I now knew that what I was doing wasn't in vain. I wasn't just keeping busy for the sake of it—I was being positioned.

God was showing me I wasn't working for people—I was working for Him.

Even when I felt unseen or underappreciated, He saw me. He never overlooked my sacrifice. Rest was just as important as work. Running myself into the ground wasn't proof of obedience—it was a sign that I needed to slow down and let Him sustain me. Isolation wasn't punishment—it was preparation. Every time I withdrew to seek Him, I came back stronger, wiser, and more confident in His plan.

One of the biggest revelations I had was that due season is not on my timeline—it's on God's. What felt like a delay was actually a divine strategy.God was orchestrating things behind the scenes. What I couldn't see was that He was aligning people, opportunities, and even my heart to be in the right place at the right time. He was protecting me from settling. If I had rushed ahead, I might have accepted less than what He had for me. His "not yet" was actually His mercy.

The seeds I was sowing were not just for me. Every act of obedience, every sacrifice, and every long day was preparing me not just for my promise, but for my purpose. I came to understand that waiting well is just as important as the promise itself. It's in the waiting that we build endurance, faith, and trust. It's in the waiting that we learn to lean on Him instead of our own strength.

As I reflect on that season, I see how God was and still is faithful. He brought me into my due season. He honored every moment of well-doing, every sacrifice, and every prayer. Marriage, motherhood, financial stability, spiritual growth—all of it came to pass in His perfect time. What I realize now is that the waiting wasn't just about receiving the promise—it was about becoming the person who could handle it. If I would have given up, settled or acted out of God's will for temporary relief or if I had allowed exhaustion to make me give up, I would have missed out on everything He had for me. I continued to hold on even when my grip felt painful and because I refused to let go; I reaped exactly what He promised.

To anyone still in their waiting season, I encourage you to keep going even

CHAPTER 7: IN DUE SEASON

when you're tired, even when you don't see results, even when doubt creeps in—keep sowing in faith. Rest. God doesn't require you to burn yourself out to prove your obedience. Rest is a part of trusting Him. Seek clarity in isolation. Don't be afraid to step away, fast, and reset. God speaks in stillness. Know that you have victory in what seems like a loss. Every long night, every lonely moment, every act of obedience—it all has purpose. You are being positioned, not forgotten. Your due season will come. If God promised it, He will do it. Your job is to not faint before the harvest arrives.

Looking back, I wouldn't change a thing. The waiting, the exhaustion, the moments of doubt—it all led me to the place I'm in now. God is faithful, and He always fulfills His promises. Hold on. Keep trusting. Your due season is on the way.

Chapter 8: A Promise Fulfilled

"Do you have any daughters of your own?"

The question was innocent enough, yet it pierced through me in a way I never expected. My best friend's daughter, a sweet and pure-hearted child who didn't know the weight those words carried, asked. "Not yet," I replied, choosing optimism over the sadness that quietly settled in my heart. "Don't worry, you'll have daughters of your own someday." Her response was immediate, filled with such conviction and certainty that my best friend and I exchanged glances—both of us surprised, though for different reasons. The statement surprised my best friend because it seemed to come out of nowhere. For me, it was something deeper. It was a prophetic moment.

The Bible tells us that "Out of the mouth of babes and sucklings, thou hast perfected praise" (Matthew 21:16). It also declares that in the last days, "your sons and daughters shall prophesy" (Acts 2:17). At that moment, I knew God was speaking to me through this child. I had heard similar words before, but this time, it resonated differently. Ministers had prophesied over me in the past, but there was something so pure and profound about hearing it from the mouth of a child. What my best friend didn't know was that, inwardly, I was struggling. I was feeling discouraged because I had not yet seen what God promised me come to fruition. I was in a season where I was doing everything right—serving, believing, trusting—still no evidence. Waiting can be one of the hardest things to do when you know God has spoken something over your life, but in His loving kindness, God saw me. He saw my hidden pain, my private prayers, my moments of wavering faith. Rather than letting me sit in my sorrow, He sent an unexpected messenger, a little girl, to remind me that His promises had not changed. That moment stayed with me. It became a memorial in my faith journey, something I could reflect on whenever doubt crept in. Whenever I felt like my waiting was for nothing, I would think back to that day in 2019 and remind myself: God is faithful. He has not forgotten me. There were other moments that sustained me on my walk. I would meet women who told me how they got married late in life and conceived multiple children in their 40's. I would see testimony after testimony of women getting married later in life and pregnant later in life.

Waiting on God is rarely easy. It stretches your faith, tests your patience, and forces you to trust when there is no visible evidence of the promise coming to pass. Abraham and Sarah's long wait for Isaac was often on my mind. I thought about Hannah, who poured out her heart in the temple, pleading for a child. I reflected on Jacob, who grappled with God, refusing release until receiving a blessing.

Like Jacob, I wasn't letting go or stop believing, but that didn't mean the journey was without struggle. There were days when the enemy whispered lies, telling me that maybe I had misheard God, that maybe the promise wasn't for me. There were moments when I saw others stepping into their season of marriage and motherhood while I remained in waiting. I was happy and rejoiced with them. I also couldn't help but wonder, God, when will it be my turn? In those moments, I had to anchor myself in God's Word. His promises are yes and amen (2 Corinthians 1:20). He is not a man that He should lie (Numbers 23:19). If He said it, He will do it. I had to believe that and believe I did. Even when it was hard and the pain seemed to overpower me.

Fast forward to the moment I found out I was pregnant. A flood of emotions overtook me—joy, gratitude, and a sense of divine fulfillment. What made it even more special was my best friend's reaction. Surprised? Not her. She reminded me of the prophecy. She reminded me of the day her daughter unknowingly spoke life into my situation, prophesying something that I had held onto for years. Now, I was walking in it. Not only was I expecting—the gender of the baby was also a girl. God had not only fulfilled His promise, but He did it in such a way that I could not deny that it was His hand at work. That was no coincidence. It wasn't luck. It was His faithfulness.

It was all a faith walk. At 40, the world tried to tell me it was too late. They filled my ears with statistics, fears, and limitations. They warned me of risks, the challenges, the impossibilities. People frequently stated that my fertility was fading. The odds were stacked against me, is what they thought. However, I do not serve a God of odds; I serve a God of miracles. I do not serve a God of limitations; I serve the Creator of life itself.

The same God who spoke the universe into existence, who breathed life into dust, who parted the sea and made a way in the wilderness—this is the God who gave me a promise. When God gives a promise, no statistic, no study, no science can stand against it. He is the Alpha and Omega, the One who opens doors no one can shut, so I chose not to listen to fear; and amplified faith. I didn't bow to doubt; I stood on His word.

With every step, I walked by faith, not by sight. I held onto His promise, knowing that when God speaks, His Word does not return to me void. Age, statistics, or human reasoning did not define my journey to marriage and motherhood. God's power defined it. Today I stand in the testimony of what He has done, living proof that faith still moves mountains, that God still keeps His promises, and that His timing is always perfect.

Today, I am witnessing God's promises manifest in my life. Every tear, every struggle, every prayer—none of it was for not. I look back on my journey and I see God's footprints in every step. There were moments of prophecy when He used even a child to remind me of His promise. Then there were the seasons of waiting, where He refined my character and deepened my trust in Him. Were there struggles? Of course. These components made the promise that much sweeter when it finally came to pass.

Some people believe in fairy tales; I choose to believe that God writes the greatest happily ever after because He is the author and finisher of my faith. Like the Israelites entering the Promised Land, I had endured a wilderness season. That time period was like being in a desert. It was long and difficult and I wondered if I would ever make it through. God brought me out and now I stand in my promise, knowing that it was worth every sacrifice.

If there is one thing I have learned through this journey, it is this: God is a promise-keeper. When we are in our most vulnerable season, He sees us. God speaks to us in ways we least expect that strengthens us when our faith wavers. He fulfills His promises in His perfect time and I am living proof of His goodness.

To those still waiting, believing, and wondering when their due season will come—I encourage you: continue to persevere. The same God who was faithful to me will be faithful to you. Continue trusting, sowing, and believing. Your promise is coming and when it does, it will be undeniable that God did it. To God be the glory. His promises are yes and amen.

www.ingramcontent.com/pod-product-compliance
Lightning Source LLC
LaVergne TN
LVHW091935070526
838200LV00068B/1268